COMMUNICATION

COMMUNICATION
SKILLS TO INSPIRE CONFIDENCE

Dr. Barrie Hopson
and Mike Scally

Johannesburg • London
San Diego • Sydney • Toronto

Published in association with

Publisher: Pfeiffer/Mercury Books

Published in the UK by Mercury Books.
This edition published by:
Pfeiffer & Company
8517 Production Avenue
San Diego, California 92121
United States of America
Editorial Offices:
(619) 578-5900, FAX (619) 578-2042
Orders:
(U.S.A.) (606) 647-3030, FAX (606) 647-3034

Copyright © 1988, 1991, 1993 by Lifeskills Learning Ltd.

Copyright under International, Pan American, and Universal Copyright Conventions. All rights reserved. No part of this book may be reproduced or transmitted in any form or by any means, electronic or mechanical, including photocopying, recording, or by any information storage-and-retrieval system, without written permission from the publisher. Brief passages (not to exceed 1,000 words) may be quoted for reviews.

This publication is designed to provide accurate and authoritative information in regard to the subject matter covered. It is sold with the understanding that the publisher is not engaged in rendering legal, accounting, or other professional service. If legal advice or other expert assistance is required, the services of a competent professional person should be sought. *From a Declaration of Principles jointly adopted by a Committee of the American Bar Association and a Committee of Publishers.*

Editor: Arlette C. Ballew
Page Compositor: Judy Whalen
Cover: John Odam Design Associates

Library of Congress Cataloging-in-Publication Data
Hopson, Barrie
  Communication: skills to inspire confidence /
Barrie Hopson and Mike Scally.
      p.   cm.
  ISBN 0-89384-211-7
  1. Interpersonal communication 2. Interpersonal
communication—Problems, exercises, etc.   I. Scally, Mike
II. Title
  BF637.C45H66 1993
  153.6–dc20   92-50990
Printed in the United States of America.
Printing 1 2 3 4 5 6 7 8 9 10

Contents

Preface	**vii**
Introduction	**1**
Objectives	2
What Is Interpersonal Communication?	2
What Would You Like to Get From This Workbook?	4
Summary	6
1 What's It For?	**7**
Personal Record Chart	8
Observer's Record Chart	10
Summary	13
2 Passing It On	**15**
Self-Talk	17
Distortion and Gossip	19
Summary	22
3 Getting It Right	**23**
The Role of the Sender	24
Checklists for the Sender	26
The Role of the Receiver	28
Checklists for the Receiver	29
Summary	31
4 It's Not What You Say, It's the Way You Say It!	**33**
The Way You Speak	34
How You Speak Checklist	35

Speaking Clearly	35
Summary	38

5 It's Not All Talk — 39

Chart: Nonverbal Clues	41
Body Posture	43
Body Posture Checklist	44
Clothes	44
Physical Setting	46
Summary	48

6 Giving and Receiving Feedback — 51

Guidelines for Giving Feedback	53
Guidelines for Receiving Feedback	55
Summary	56

7 Discussions and Arguments: Managing Conflict — 57

How Do You Feel About Conflict?	59
What Are the Causes of Conflict?	60
Conflict Resolution	62
The Five Skills of Negotiation	63
The Check-It-Out Questionnaire	67
Summary	69

8 Making Contact — 71

Option 1	72
Observer's Communication Checklist	73
Option 2	75
Option 3	76
Summary	78

Action Plan	**81**
About the Authors	**83**

Preface

Welcome to our series of open learning workbooks. In this brief preface, we invite you to consider some of our beliefs:

- **We do not need teachers to learn.** Not all of what we know in life was learned through formal education. We can, and do, learn in a wide range of ways, and we learn best when we know our own needs.
- **The best way to help people is to encourage them to help themselves.** Self-help and self-management avoid the dependency that blocks development and burdens ourselves and others.
- **Awareness, knowledge, and skills give us more options in life.** Lack of any of these is a disadvantage; possession of them allows us to live fuller lives, shaping events rather than simply reacting.
- **The more able and accomplished we become, the more we fill society's reservoir of talent and contribute to the common good.**
- **It has been said that the future is not what it used to be!** In this age, the goalposts keep being moved, so increasingly our security needs to come from having information and skills.

The term "lifeskill" came from work based on these beliefs, which we began at Leeds University in the 1970s. Our philosophy has been widely applied in education, in industry and commerce, and in the community, inviting people to take charge of their lives and make them satisfying and rewarding.

Lifeskills have, so far, been available through training courses and teaching programs. Now they are available in a self-help format that is consistent with the Lifeskills approach, because you are in charge of your own learning. Learn at your own pace, in your own time, and apply your learning to your situation. We wish you enjoyment and success!

Barrie Hopson
Mike Scally

Introduction

This book is for people who care about pursuing self-development. It involves reading and doing, so we have written it as an open learning workbook.

Open learning describes a study program that is designed to adapt to the needs of individual learners. Some open learning programs involve attendance at a study center of some kind, or contact with a tutor or mentor, but even then attendance times are flexible and suit the individual. This workbook is for you to use at home or at work. Most of the activities are for you to complete alone. Sometimes we may suggest that you talk with a friend or colleague—self-development is easier if there is another person with whom to talk over ideas. But this isn't essential by any means.

With this workbook you can

- Organize your study to suit your own needs.
- Study the material alone or with other people.
- Work through the book at your own pace.
- Start and finish just when and where you want to, although we have indicated suggested stopping points with a ☕ symbol.

The sections marked "Personal Project" involve you in more than working through the text; they require you to take additional time—sometimes an evening, sometimes a week.

For this reason, we do not suggest specifically how long it will take you to complete this workbook, but the written part of the book will probably take you about six hours to complete.

Objectives

In this introduction we shall explore what we mean by interpersonal communication. Chapter 1 looks at the purpose of communication. The other five chapters look at the practical skills needed to communicate effectively and offer you opportunities to identify and practice the skills you would like to develop.

Our objectives in this self-help program are to identify

- The part played by face-to-face communication in our lives.
- Factors that interfere with effective communication.
- Skills that contribute to effective communication.
- Speaking skills that contribute to good communication.
- The part played by nonverbal factors in one-to-one communication.
- The skills needed to give and receive feedback.
- The skills of negotiation and managing conflict.
- And to practice face-to-face communication skills.

What Is Interpersonal Communication?

A great deal of our lives is spent in communication. We are influenced in many ways by the communication systems we call the media: newspapers, radio, and television. We also spend a considerable amount of time in contact with other people. Each of these contacts involves communication— talking, arguing, exchanging ideas, chatting, listening, giving information, voicing our opinions and feelings, and so on. Most communication happens without individuals being very conscious of what is going on between them. If the communication is good we will probably benefit, but if it is not so good we may run into problems. We have all heard the phrases "lack of communication" and "communication breakdown."

This book is subtitled *Skills to Inspire Confidence* because it concentrates on the interpersonal communication skills that take place between people who are talking face to face. This sort of communicating is something that each of us begins to do normally from the time we are born. We learn to speak as we learn to walk, to play, and to dress ourselves, so it is tempting to assume that our communication skills come to us as part of our natural development. Yet some people develop into very effective communicators while others barely reach survival level.

Why are communication skills important? Without communication there would be no relationships. Sharing ideas, giving opinions, finding out what we need to know, explaining what we want, working out differences with others, and expressing our feelings are all examples of the kind of face-to-face communication that is essential if we are to relate to and work with other people.

Good managers know that the key to effective management lies in successfully managing people and relationships, not production figures. Good communication is the cornerstone of a successful enterprise. Experts have shown that most people spend more time communicating with other people than in any other activity, including production. When communication fails, production breaks down.

The following diagram describes what happens when two people talk to each other face to face.

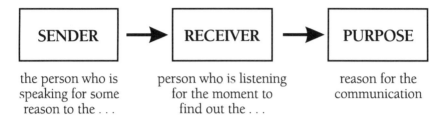

SENDER	RECEIVER	PURPOSE
the person who is speaking for some reason to the ...	person who is listening for the moment to find out the ...	reason for the communication

In most conversations, we continually move backward and forward between the roles of sender and receiver, rather like the ball in a game of tennis.

What makes a good communicator? The qualities that help us to communicate effectively are

- **Respect:** making people feel valued and important;
- **Honesty:** coming across as genuine, not being pretentious or playing games; and
- **Empathy:** trying to see things from the other person's point of view.

These qualities are the foundation on which to build and develop the communication skills we will explore in this program.

What Would You Like to Get From This Workbook?

Before you move on, what have you discovered so far about interpersonal or face-to-face communication? See if you can answer the following questions.

List three characteristics of face-to-face communication.

1 _____
2 _____
3 _____

INTRODUCTION 5

Now think of three examples of communication that do not involve face-to-face contact.

1 _____
2 _____
3 _____

You might have said that face-to-face communication involves

- Contact with other people through conversation and discussion.
- Sharing ideas, opinions, information, and feelings.
- Relating to and working with other people.
- Sending and receiving messages to achieve a purpose.

Your list of examples that *don't* involve face-to-face communication might include radio, television, newspaper advertisements, application forms, telephone calls, correspondence, and so on.

What are the advantages of being able to communicate well with other people? Write down one of the general advantages we have mentioned and then think about the personal benefits to you.

If *we* communicate well we can _____
_____
_____

If *I* communicate well it will help me to _____
_____
_____

Summary

We hope that what you have read so far will help you identify specific personal objectives or advantages that you would like to achieve through this program. We suggest that you write them down here and use them to help you to decide which parts of the program will be most helpful to you.

By the end of this program I would like to be able to

_____
_____
_____
_____

1

What's It For?

The objective of this chapter is to identify the part played by face-to-face communication in our lives.

Think about the amount of face-to-face communication that takes place every day of our lives. Use the chart below to fill in your own personal record of a typical day. Spend about ten minutes filling in the chart. Enter details about the communication contacts you had with other people.

Personal Record Chart

Communication record for _____ day		
People Involved	**Purpose**	**Results**

Your notes may look something like this:

Sample Personal Record Chart

Communication record for _____ day		
People Involved	**Purpose**	**Results**
Me–daughter	To find out why she didn't get home by 10:00.	Agreed she'll telephone me next time she is late.
Me–boss	To agree to most convenient day to have off next week.	Agreed to take Thursday off.
Me–plumber	To arrange visit Thursday morning to fix sink pipe.	Agreed to come at 9:00.
Me–secretary	To rearrange two appointments scheduled for next Thursday.	Secretary made arrangements.
Me–client no. 1	To discuss contract.	Contract agreed.
Me–client no. 2	To go through queries about contract.	Queries answered.
Me–kids	To tell we'll go to the circus on Thursday.	Ecstatic screams.
Me–ex-husband	Negotiate which of us has the kids this weekend.	Terrible argument; usual problem.

Personal Project

Try to observe examples of conversations between other people in the same way. Ask family members, friends, or colleagues to allow you to observe them. With their agreement, keep a record of their face-to-face communications over one day. Use the chart on the next page to record these conversations, the purpose of them, and the results. At the end of the day, sit down with the people involved, show them your record, and discuss what you have written. It is interesting—and sometimes surprising—to note the differences between their perceptions of what went on and yours. Jot down the discrepancies, and why you think they occurred, in the space below the chart.

Observer's Record Chart

Communication record for _____ day		
People Involved	**Purpose**	**Results**

Were there any discrepancies in perception?
_____
_____

Why do you think these happened?
_____
_____

Now that you have recorded some detailed examples of face-to-face communication, think about the general purpose of communicating.

Why do people communicate? Write down at least four general reasons based on the purpose columns of your lists.

1 _____
2 _____
3 _____
4 _____

People communicate for many reasons, including to

- Inform
- Find out
- Learn
- Persuade
- Cooperate
- Amuse or entertain
- Negotiate
- Supervise or direct
- Help or support

Each of us spends many hours of each day communicating with others. In fact, *several years* of our lives will be spent in this activity. If we communicate *well,* we are likely to be successful in many of our endeavors. If we do not communicate well, we could miss out on many opportunities.

Now think about the possible results of good and bad communication. Spend about five minutes on each section, writing down as many results of good or bad communication as you can think of.

If we communicate *well* we will be able to _____
_____
_____
_____

If we communicate *badly* it could mean _____ _____
__ _____
_____
_____

Personal Project

Over the next week, observe people closely until you see one example of really good communication and one example of really bad communication. Write down what the senders and receivers were doing in each case. A word of warning: Don't watch people too closely. In many cultures, staring at people is interpreted as bad communication!

An example of *good* communication
_____
_____
_____

An example of *bad* communication
_____
_____
_____

Good communicators are likely to find life more satisfying and more rewarding. In the next few pages, we look at and practice the skills you need to communicate well.

Summary

Good communication brings obvious benefits. We can influence others, learn more, get more of what we want, develop better relationships, settle differences, help others, and even make the world a better place!

Poor communication is likely to cause difficulties. Relationships will be poor, learning will be harder, other people will find us confusing, we will be unable to achieve our ambitions, we will be unlikely to be able to help others, and we probably will find life frustrating and unfulfilling.

2

Passing It On

The objective of this chapter is to identify factors that interfere with face-to-face communication.

When we are listening to another person, even when we think that we are concentrating, the message that we "hear" is likely to be affected by many factors. If we pass the message on, we may change it substantially, even if we do not do so knowingly. This change in the message is known as *distortion*.

Think back over the last week. Can you think of an example from your personal relationships of communication that has become distorted? Use the space below to describe the situation. Try to suggest reasons why the message was distorted.

The situation was _____
_____
_____
_____

The message was distorted because _____
_____
_____
_____

If you have young children, you may have thought of an occasion when you were distracted during a conversation by having to attend to a child's needs. Alternatively, you may have been worried or anxious about something and lost your concentration; perhaps you were impatient to put in your point of view and did not listen; perhaps you simply "switched off" because you were bored.

Self-Talk

You may also have thought of an example of an interaction with a partner in which "wires crossed"; you both thought you had a clear idea of what was said, but each had quite different interpretations of it. This happens all the time in all kinds of communication, particularly in communication that involves feelings. It is very easy to allow our own feelings to get in the way of hearing what the other person is trying to say, and, of course, the other person may have similar interference operating at the same time. Add to this the fact that we do not always check out what has been said (because we assume that we have been understood) and the result is a scenario of so many possible complications that it seems amazing that we understand one another at all!

One of the factors that affects this sort of communication is self-talk. Shut your eyes for a few seconds and try not to think of anything in particular. Try to empty your mind.

You will have found (unless you are trained to make your mind a blank) that your head is full of pictures, words, sounds, snatches of sentences, and sensations. This babble goes on all the time. Your brain "talks" to you constantly about the world around you; it filters a jumble of impressions and makes sense of it in your own terms. Most of the time, you are unaware of your brain's activity, but without it your thoughts would be just a confusion of sights, sounds, and sensations with no meaning, similar to when you tried to empty your mind.

We do not react directly to situations. Our senses take everything in, then our brains pick out the things that are relevant to the situation and what we feel about it. As a result of this self-talk, we react.

The sequence of events is always:

Sometimes, when your self-talk is positive, it will work for you; but when the self-talk is negative, it will work against you. If you tell yourself, on one of those bad days we all have, that you feel as if everything will go wrong for you, the chances are that everything will. You are likely to feel negative and defensive, which means that you will look unfriendly and grumpy; this will show in your posture and on your face, and other people's reactions to you will be negative as a result. In addition to that, you may only hear the "bad" in what other people say. A typical example of this is a woman who buys a new dress and comes home to show it to her husband. He likes it and says so, meaning to be as complimentary as he can. He thinks the color is just right and that it makes her look really slim. She does not hear the compliment but pounces on the remark about it making her look slim and accuses him of implying that she usually looks fat. Is this kind of interchange at all familiar? We all do it at some time, whether it is about new clothes, an important piece of work, our cooking, our tidiness—the list is endless.

We can control our own self-talk and, consequently, eliminate this kind of distortion. Once we are aware of our own favorite negative messages, we can control them.

One technique is to say **STOP!** out loud to yourself when you catch yourself being negative. Then immediately substitute a positive statement and repeat it to yourself. It helps to have some positive statements ready. Think of positive messages to use when you hear negative messages in your self-talk and write them down here. Now memorize each one and substitute the positive statement for the negative message. This technique sounds a bit silly, but it really does work!

1. Your own familiar negative message

_____

Your positive statement

_____

2. Your negative message

_____

Your positive statement

_____

3. Your negative message

_____

Your positive statement

_____

Can you think of any other reasons for distortion? The next task will help you to identify them.

Distortion and Gossip

Personal Project

Watch an episode of a television program or look for real-life situations in which one person tells a story or passes on a piece of information or "gossip" to another. Try to observe two or three of these occasions and use the questions below to help you make notes about them.

How does the message change when it is passed on?

1 _____
2 _____
3 _____

What reasons can you think of for the distortion of the message?

1 _____
2 _____
3 _____

Your reasons might have included some of the following points:

- Having to listen when there are distractions around can cause us to miss things.
- If we like the person, we are more likely to listen than if we dislike them; *who* tells us something makes a difference.
- If we have to think of other things, or have other things on our mind, it is difficult to listen well.
- If people are excited, tense, or confused, and do not speak clearly, it is more difficult to pick up the message.

Personal Project

Here is another task to work through that will help you to identify other factors that affect communication. You will need a cassette recorder or video recorder and a blank tape for this task.

Listen to a news program on the television or radio and record it onto audio or video tape. Choose a short piece from the broadcast and imagine that you are going to retell it to another person. Record *your* account of the story on tape or by writing it down. Then replay the original broadcast and compare this report with your version of the story.

Have the facts changed significantly (or slightly)?
_____
_____

Write down two or three reasons that are different from the ones you gave above for the distortion of the story.

1 _____
2 _____
3 _____

Did your reasons include any of the following?

- Having to listen to a great deal of information can cause us to pick up only part of it.
- If the subject bores us, we do not listen as attentively as if the subject is interesting.
- If what we listen to is too technical or full of unknown words, we become frustrated.
- If we do not want to listen or be involved, we "turn off our attention."

To get some idea of how effectively you communicate, you need to involve another person in your activities. You might ask a friend, a member of your family, or someone at work to act as your partner.

Now repeat the news story task with your partner. Record a news broadcast on audio or video tape. Choose an item from the news and retell it to your partner, asking him or her to write down the main facts of the story. Then compare these notes with the recording of the news. How close are they?

Circle the most appropriate word:

My partner's checklist included	**all**	
	most	of the main facts
	some	of the story
	none	

How well do you think you performed as a receiver in the tasks? It is likely that most of the points you listed as reasons for distortion were related to your role as a receiver. The tasks emphasized the importance of good *listening* skills for effective communication.

Summary

You have begun to make a list of factors that hinder communication—a list of things to avoid. Knowing what can go wrong is the first step in identifying the factors that will *help* communication.

Before going on to the next chapter, try to spend some time observing people talking and listening to one another. Over the next few days, notice what people around you do that helps or hinders the messages that flow between them.

3

Getting It Right

The objective of this chapter is to identify those factors that will help to make face-to-face communication more effective, i.e., the skills of sending and receiving interpersonal messages.

Did you remember to watch people talking and listening to one another? What did you notice? Write a few notes about what you observed in the space below.

The Role of the Sender

You have already looked at some of the factors that can interfere with good communication. The following task builds on the work you did in the previous activity to enable you to produce some guidelines for good communication.

Personal Project

Watch one or two current affairs discussion programs or interviews on television. Concentrate on the role of the sender. (This may be the interviewer or the person who is presenting his or her case first.) It is probably easier if you focus on one aspect at a time, e.g., things that *help* sending. Then move on to watch for those things that *hinder* sending. Make a list of DOs and DON'Ts in the boxes below.

DOs (things that *help* sending)

DON'Ts (things that *hinder* sending)

Did your list of DOs and DON'Ts include any of the ones on the following checklists? Make a check mark in the boxes next to the statements that correspond to your own.

Checklists for the Sender

DOs

☐ Be clear about what you want to say. If you are not, you may confuse the receiver by changing your message halfway through or by getting sidetracked.

☐ Look at the receiver. Making eye contact is very important when you are trying to get your point across. (This is mentioned in Chapter 4 in the discussion of body language.) Looking everywhere but at the receiver gives the impression that you are being evasive or untruthful or are uninterested.

☐ Speak clearly. This seems obvious, but it is easy to forget when you are concentrating on what you are saying. You may speak too quickly or mumble so that you cannot be heard properly.

☐ Consider the feelings of the receiver. To be a good communicator, you need to try to put yourself in the receiver's place so that he or she feels that you are talking directly to him or her, and so that you can make your points relevant.

☐ Make sure that your words match your tone and body language. There is more on this in Chapter 4.

☐ Check that the receiver has understood what you have said. For instance, summarize from time to time, or occasionally ask questions to make sure that the receiver understands what you are saying.

☐ Vary the tone and pace at which you speak so that your voice is interesting to listen to. Talking in a monotone can put your receiver to sleep! There is more on this in Chapter 4.

DON'Ts

☐ Don't complicate what you are saying with too much detail or difficult language. Remember that what you are saying is new to the receiver, and he or she needs to have it presented so that it can be followed easily.

☐ Don't talk so much that the receiver has no chance to comment or to ask questions. A receiver needs to be able to do this in order to understand what is being said and to feel valued.

☐ Don't be vague; give concrete examples of what you mean.

☐ Don't ridicule or attack your receiver.

☐ If you want the receiver to listen to what you are saying, you must show that you respect him or her.

☐ Don't use particular ideas that you know will irritate the receiver. A person will not be able to listen to you if you do not show respect for his or her values.

☐ Don't ignore signs of confusion, resentment, or disinterest. If the receiver is confused, resentful, or uninterested, he or she will not hear what you have to say.

☐ Don't speak in a detached, remote way. If you do, it will seem to the receiver that you are not interested in what you are saying. (Therefore, why should it be interesting to the receiver?) Or it may seem that you are not interested in really communicating to the receiver.

☐ Don't pretend or exaggerate. If you do, you will devalue what you are trying to communicate. It is also very annoying for the receiver.

Looking at the list of DOs and DON'Ts for the sender, do you see any examples that relate to you—that you would like to note and work on? Just being aware of them will help you to counteract them. Jot down one thing you need to watch out for and one thing you do well.

I need to watch out for _____

_____

I am good at _____

_____

The Role of the Receiver

Listening skills are just as important in communication as sending skills. Listening is not the same as hearing. It is a common mistake to confuse the two, to think that if you are able to hear, you are able to listen and do not need to develop your listening skills.

Personal Project

This project is similar to the one you did for the role of the sender. Watch one or two current-affairs discussion programs or interviews on television. This time, concentrate on the role of the receiver. Again, it is probably easier if you focus first on the things that seem to be helpful and then on the things that are not helpful.

DOs

DON'Ts

Now compare your DOs and DON'Ts with the ones in the checklists that follow. Make a check mark in the boxes next to the statements that correspond to your own.

Checklists for the Receiver

DOs

- ☐ Look at the person who is speaking to you to show that you are listening and are interested in what he or she is saying.

- ☐ Recognize how the speaker feels about what he or she is saying. If you can put yourself in the speaker's place, you will be able to understand what the speaker means to say.

- ☐ Look for points to agree with rather than to argue with. You may stop the speaker prematurely by taking issue with points and arguing.

- ☐ Give a quick summary of what you have heard every now and then to check out that you have heard correctly. As we have seen in Chapter 2, distortion can happen as a result of all manner of occurrences.

- ☐ Give full attention to the speaker by facing him or her and using nods and comments to show that you are listening. This is not just a matter of courtesy and respect for the speaker; it also encourages him or her to continue.

DON'Ts

☐ Don't interrupt the speaker to give your views (interrupting the flow of what you are being told).

☐ Don't start thinking about something else and get distracted. The speaker will soon realize that you are not listening and will be discouraged. You also will lose the flow and miss what is being said.

☐ Don't let your previous experience of the person deter you. This does not mean that you shouldn't take what you know of the speaker into consideration, but you should try not to write off what is being said because of your view of the speaker; he or she might have something valid to contribute (and you may change your opinion).

☐ Don't let prejudices get in the way of what is being said. Stay aware of your prejudices: they may sneak up on you. If you know that a particular subject is a touchy one for you, check your reactions carefully as you go.

☐ Don't be negative about, or belittle, what the speaker is saying. This does not mean that you shouldn't disagree with the speaker, just that you should avoid evaluative and insulting remarks. Show respect for the speaker's point of view.

☐ Don't change the subject. Obviously, this is not going to help you to hear what is being said (or what might have been said!).

☐ Don't fidget or distract the speaker. This can be extremely offputting for anyone, especially if what the speaker is saying is difficult to express.

Look through this list of DOs and DON'Ts for the receiver and make a note in the space that follows of one thing you need to watch out for and one thing you do well.

I need to watch out for _____

_____

I am good at _____

_____

Summary

Do you feel more confident about your skills as a sender or as a receiver? People often are better at one role than the other. Think how often you have heard the comment, "She's a good listener." If you find that people often come to talk to you about their problems, the chances are that you are skillful at listening and receiving messages. If people often come to you for advice or opinions, or ask you to speak to other people on their behalf, you probably are skillful at sending messages. Decide which of the two roles you most need to work on at the moment. (If you find this difficult, ask a friend or colleague where he or she thinks your strengths lie.)

I think I am more successful at sending because

_____

_____

I think I am more successful at receiving because

_____

_____

I would like to develop my skill as a sender because

_____

_____

I would like to develop my skill as a receiver because
_____
_____

Look back over the points in the checklist for either the sender or the receiver. Choose three points that you think you need to work on.

Below are three steps that I can take in the next week to improve my skills as a sender/receiver.

1 _____
2 _____
3 _____

4

It's Not What You Say, It's the Way You Say It!

The objective of this chapter is to identify the part played by tone of voice and general use of voice in one-to-one communication and to suggest ways of developing techniques to improve the voice.

How do you estimate your ability to use your voice? Do you tend to speak too quietly or too quickly? Do you vary the tone and pitch of your voice?

The Way You Speak

If you can get hold of a recording machine, record yourself having a conversation with someone or simply say a few words into the machine and play it back. If you are not used to hearing yourself on tape, it can be a shock. You can sound quite different from the way you think you do.

How do you sound? First, check with another person that the recording does accurately represent your normal speaking voice. Sometimes nervousness about being recorded can cause you to speak differently.

Bearing in mind what the other person has said, use the following checklist to analyze your voice, putting a check mark next to the things you hear yourself doing. You will then have an idea of what you might want to improve.

How You Speak Checklist

☐ Do you pronounce each word distinctly?

☐ Do you speak too fast to be understood?

☐ Do you speak too slowly to keep people's attention?

☐ Do you run all your words together, not leaving enough time in between each one?

☐ Do you sound sincere?

☐ Do you sound too loud?

☐ Do you sound too quiet?

☐ Does your voice sound shrill or squeaky?

☐ Does your voice sound monotonous?

☐ Does your tone convey how you feel?

How did you do? Unless you have been trained to use your voice properly, you probably will have found one or two things you could work on. Read through the following pages, paying particular attention to discussions of the areas in which you feel you need to improve.

Speaking Clearly

Nervousness and habit are the culprits here. Your speech might be blurred as a result of clenching your jaw as you speak. (This is a common nervous habit.)

Tighten your jaw, with your mouth half closed, and say "clear diction is an asset," moving your clenched jaw as little as possible. Now unclench it, relax it by moving it up and down a few times, and say the same sentence again, moving your mouth and jaw freely. Can you hear the difference?

Accent

Most people speak with an accent of some sort, either regional or national, which is regarded as acceptable and sometimes desirable. However, it has not been considered good for radio and television presenters to have accents, because they need to be understood by their audiences. Therefore, they have to speak without a noticeable accent. Even that is now changing, as long as they say their words clearly and are understood.

Speed

The speed at which you talk generally is affected by what you are talking about and how you feel about it. If you are excited, you will speak more quickly; if you are bored, you will slow down. You can convey urgency and importance by speeding up, but if you speak quickly all the time, the urgency will be lost—and so will the clarity. Again, nervousness might make you talk quickly and not as clearly, so be aware when you are doing this and speak more slowly. Remember that slow speech also is difficult to listen to. You may be pronouncing every word perfectly, but the chances are that you will put your listener to sleep. However, this is not a very common problem.

Tone

Your tone is a vital part of how you convey your message. You can sound sincere, enthusiastic, or annoyed; your tone can tell the listener what you think of him or her; it also can tell the listener how you feel about what you are talking about and can affect his or her judgment of what you're saying.

You can make the same word mean several things. Try saying the word "good" and make it sound:

- Bored
- Sarcastic
- Pleased
- Overjoyed
- Angry
- Surprised
- Sincere
- Hurried

The most important thing to remember is *appropriateness.* If your tone is appropriate to what you are saying, how you feel about it, and how you feel about your listener, you are using your tone well. It is very easy to allow your voice to give you away and convey tiredness or irritation when those things are inappropriate to the situation—or to the person you are talking to. It can be quite upsetting to be snapped at for no apparent reason because someone is irritated about something else entirely. Be sure you watch out for this situation and make sure it doesn't happen.

Volume

Speaking too quietly to be heard can be an indication of nervousness. If you tend to do this, practice speaking with your chin up and try to reach the person farthest from you. Volume control relies on good, deep, regular breathing, which often becomes quick and shallow when you are nervous. Always take a few deep breaths prior to speaking.

Varying the volume of your voice, provided it is not too extreme, can add interest to what you are saying. However, take care not to sound too theatrical.

Pitch

The pitch of your voice—whether it is high or low (deep)—often is affected by nervousness, fear, or tension. Your throat muscles and your vocal cords tighten, and the sound becomes squeaky or shrill.

If this happens to you, practice by taking a deep breath and, as you breathe out slowly, say a few short words such as "I want to talk." Your voice will automatically sound better, as it is physically impossible to breathe out and keep your muscles tight at the same time.

Summary

In this chapter, we have explored the ways in which our voices can be used, that is, the words we use and the ways of delivering those words.

The next chapter concentrates on another important aspect of communication that is not always obvious, but that is certainly essential.

5

It's Not All Talk

The objective of this chapter is to identify the part played by nonverbal factors in one-to-one communication.

Normally we think that communication involves words, but this is not necessarily so. People can also communicate *without* words.

Nonverbal communication is the act of passing messages between people in ways that do not employ words. Some experts say that up to 75 percent of what is conveyed between people is communicated without using speech.

We receive nonverbal messages from many different sources: facial expressions; the way in which people sit, stand, or move; where people stand or sit in relation to one another; how we hold and move our hands, arms, legs, and torso; and so on. Whether we are aware of it or not, we are sending and receiving nonverbal signals almost all the time. The words that we use to communicate to one another are important, but it is just as important to be aware of what nonverbal signals we use to communicate to others—and what our signals communicate about us.

Faces can show many different expressions. Write down three emotions that faces can convey.

1 _____
2 _____
3 _____

Some possible answers are bored, happy, sad, angry, or surprised.

Whenever we communicate face to face with other people, we unconsciously notice their expressions and movements and form impressions about them on the basis of those behaviors. These behaviors give us clues about people. If we learn to read those clues carefully and skillfully, we can learn a good deal about others —without any verbal communication at all.

The following are some examples of the kinds of behavior that give us nonverbal clues. In the right-hand column, write the possible meanings that might be in each clue.

Nonverbal Clues

Clue	Possible Meaning(s)
• Nodding the head	
• Shaking the head slowly/quickly	
• Turning the face away	
• Facing you with eyes down or looking away	
• Staring eyes/glaring eyes	
• Slight smile	
• Lips tightly closed	
• Jaw dropped open	
• Deep breath	
• Sigh	
• Broad smile	
• Soft voice	
• Loud voice	
• Shaky/hesitant voice	

Note in the spaces below what you have discovered from this activity about how we use our faces and heads to communicate with one another.

How clear are the meanings of nonverbal clues?
_____
_____

What do you think is the most expressive part of the body?
_____
_____

How do we use our eyes to communicate?
_____
_____

We noted the following points:

1. There is likely to be a variety of meanings for each clue. The head and face can communicate an enormous range of nonverbal messages. Because of this, we sometimes can attach the wrong meaning to the nonverbal clues we get from other people. Assumptions made about other people can often be wrong. We need to check our perceptions by asking questions.
2. The face is probably the most expressive part of the body, telling us a great deal about a person. The main messages it carries are usually happiness, surprise, sadness, fear, anger, disgust, contempt, or interest. The eyes and mouth signal many of our feelings, and observing the face when we talk to another person is our most useful "second channel," giving extra meaning to the person's words. Head nods tell the speaker to continue. A rapid head nod might convey agreement or be a signal to hurry up and finish speaking.

3. Eye contact is very important. It shows that we are in contact with each other, it gives us signals about the other person's feelings, and it enables us to signal to the other person to start or to stop talking. It is especially important in the receiver. Unless the person to whom we are speaking looks at us, we are likely to think he or she is not listening.

There are other ways we can communicate with one another without words:

- Body posture
- Clothes
- Physical setting

We will look at each of these in turn.

Body Posture

A person's posture can tell us a good deal about his or her feelings. The way in which a person sits, stands, moves, and walks can signal whether he or she is relaxed, happy, dejected, nervous, or angry. We use our hands and arms unconsciously to give added meaning to what we say. We use them to emphasize points and to demonstrate feelings.

Personal Project

Over the next three days, look carefully at the ways in which other people hold and move their bodies (including their hands, arms, and legs) when they are communicating. Stop to look at your own body positions from time to time. When you observe an example of the body positions described in the chart on the next page, place a check mark next to it. In the right-hand column, make notes about the message(s) you think the position conveys.

Body Posture Checklist

Body Position	Observed	Possible Meaning(s)
• Slumping in a chair	☐	
• Sitting upright on the edge of a chair	☐	
• Sitting and leaning toward the other person	☐	
• Sitting with arms folded and legs crossed	☐	
• Sitting with arms and hands relaxed and legs slightly apart	☐	
• Hands clenched tightly	☐	
• Hands open, arms reaching toward the other person	☐	
• Pacing back and forth	☐	
• Shrugging shoulders	☐	
• Wringing hands	☐	
• Fiddling with keys or pencil	☐	
• Sitting still, relaxed, and looking at the other person	☐	
• Leaning back on chair with hands behind head	☐	

Clothes

What can we tell about a person from the clothes that he or she wears? Some experts suggest that we form impressions of people within four seconds of meeting them, and that 60 percent of the impression is based on appearance! The other 40 percent is based on speech.

Answer the following questions to get a sense of the different messages that clothes can communicate.

What kind of clothes do you feel comfortable in?
_____
_____

If you have a job, what kind of clothes do you wear at work?
_____
_____

What kind of clothes does your boss wear?
_____
_____

What kind of clothes would you wear to a job interview?
_____
_____

Are there any other clothes that another person might wear that you would find off-putting or unfriendly? Are there any that you would find friendly?
_____
_____

How much are clothes a reliable guide to what a person is really like?
_____
_____

Clothes are likely to have different meanings in different settings. You may, for example, feel comfortable in jeans, and jeans are acceptable for shopping at the mall, but you probably wouldn't wear them to a job interview. Similarly, formal evening wear is out of place at the supermarket or the office.

The clothes that we wear at home or at work are likely to reflect the "uniform" of the social group to which we belong. We tend to look for and recognize this uniform in other people. We may take less notice of, or even dislike, someone who is obviously wearing a different "uniform."

Some experts suggest that we are more likely to be successful at job interviews if we "dress up" and wear the uniform of someone in the tier above our present position.

Clothes may not be a reliable guide to what a person is actually like. What someone is wearing doesn't really tell us how punctual or efficient he or she is, how caring he or she might be, or how much money he or she has. You may even believe that it is unfair or superficial to judge a person by the clothes he or she wears. But the overwhelming evidence is that what we wear and how we wear it make a difference. Clothes that are inappropriate for the circumstances will get in the way of what we want to communicate.

Physical Setting

The way that we arrange ourselves and our furniture in the space that we occupy also conveys important nonverbal messages. Think of some office spaces that you have been in. What did the physical setting tell you about the relationship between the people?

Observe people around you when they are in conversation. Is there an ideal distance or position that makes talking easy?

There are, of course, important cultural differences in the ways in which people use physical space and organize their physical settings. In some Western countries, outside the home there is generally little physical contact between people. Unless they are very friendly, a handshake may be the only acceptable form of making contact, especially between men.

Being too far apart or too close makes conversation difficult. For example, the most acceptable distance in Anglo-Saxon cultures is about two and one-half feet. If people stand or sit too close to one another, they are likely to feel uncomfortable. Test this while you are talking to someone by moving closer than you normally would. The other person will almost certainly move away.

Two people who are communicating at a table are likely to use the following positions:

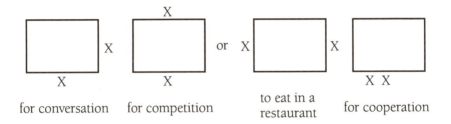

Physical barriers between people, such as desks and tables, are likely to suggest separation and distance in the relationship. Being behind a desk, sitting on a higher chair, or standing over somebody can give a person a position of power. Think about how you can apply these observations in the way you use your own space.

If someone were to come into your room, and you wanted to make the person feel uncomfortable, how could you arrange yourself and the other person to do that?

_____
_____
_____

If you wanted someone to feel comfortable and welcome, how could you arrange that?

_____

_____

_____

If a stranger visited your home, what might he or she know about you just by looking around your living room?

_____

_____

_____

Summary

From these activities, you will have discovered that nonverbal communication can help you in making contact with other people. You will be sending signals about yourself, whether you are aware of it or not. How you dress, sit, stand, and walk will tell other people about you, so it is important to be aware of the messages you want to give and how you want to give them. Also, you want to make sure that you are not sending one message with your words and another with your face and body!

As you communicate, you are likely to be able to tell from the other person's face how your message is being received—whether your ideas and questions are being listened to, understood, agreed with, and so on. You can observe when you might need to repeat or rephrase something, when it might be better to withdraw, and what effect your spoken words are having on the listener's feelings.

As a listener or receiver, you will need to be aware of using nonverbal signals that show interest: eye contact, nodding, appropriate facial expressions, turning toward the speaker, leaning forward if you are sitting down, and so on.

Your body is always communicating. Remember, the effective signals in talking and listening to someone are

- Facing the person
- Having an open posture
- Leaning toward the person
- Keeping good eye contact
- Being relaxed

Now consider how you can apply what you have discovered about nonverbal communication in your day-to-day interaction with people.

Three things I can do to improve the ways I communicate other than in words are

1 _____
2 _____
3 _____

6

Giving and Receiving Feedback

The objective of this chapter is to identify skills needed to give and receive feedback in a constructive way.

People give us feedback by telling us how they feel about our work, about our attitude, or about comments we have made. Feedback is a way of learning more about ourselves and the effect that our behavior has on others. If feedback is constructive and given skillfully, it increases self-awareness and encourages personal development. If feedback is destructive or given in an unskilled way, it simply leaves the person who is receiving it feeling bad and with no concrete goals for improvement.

This does not mean to say that all constructive feedback must be positive. Negative feedback, given skillfully, also can be useful and important for our development.

Think about an occasion when you have received feedback that you found positive and helpful. Describe the situation and try to give reasons that you found it constructive.

One occasion when I received helpful feedback was _____
_____
_____

I found it constructive because _____
_____
_____

If your feelings about receiving feedback were positive, it is likely that the person giving it was skillful and used some of the following guidelines. See if you recognize any of them.

Guidelines for Giving Feedback

1. **Be clear about what you want to say in advance. Start with the positive.**

    Most people need encouragement, to be told when they are doing something well. When you offer feedback it helps the recipient to hear first what you appreciate in him or her or what he or she has done well.

2. **Be specific.**

    Avoid general comments that are not very useful when it comes to developing skills. If you use statements such as "You were brilliant" or "It was awful," state *specifically* what was done that led you to say what you did. Select priority areas.

3. **Refer to behaviors that can be changed.**

    It is not helpful to give a person feedback about something he or she has no control over. For example, people can improve their posture but they cannot change their height.

4. **Offer alternatives.**

    If you do offer negative feedback, do not simply criticize but also suggest what the person could have done differently. After explaining the error, offer the correct way or perhaps a better way of handling the matter.

5. **Be descriptive rather than evaluative.**

    Tell the person what you saw or heard and the effect it had on you, rather than merely saying something was just "good" or "bad."

6. "Own" the feedback.

It is important that responsibility is taken for the feedback that is offered. Beginning the feedback with "I" or "In my opinion" is a way of avoiding the impression of voicing a universally agreed opinion.

7. Leave the recipient with a choice.

Skilled feedback offers people information about themselves in a way that leaves them with a choice of whether to act on it or not.

8. Think about what the feedback says about you.

Feedback is likely to say as much about the giver as it does about the receiver. It will say a good deal about the giver's values and what he or she focuses on in others.

9. Give the feedback as soon as you can after the event.

Keeping comments current keeps them relevant. A past event may have been superseded by an event that makes our original feedback meaningless or dated. It is important that feedback be timely.

Each of us is in the position of giving feedback to another person more frequently than first imagined. It may be to a child, a partner, or a friend in our home life, or to a colleague at work.

Think about a recent occasion when you gave someone feedback. Was the situation at home, at work, or somewhere else?

_____
_____

What was your relationship to the person?

_____
_____

After reading through the preceding guidelines, do you think that the feedback you gave was constructive? Why?

_____
_____

Which points could you work on to improve in the future?

_____
_____

If we are on the receiving end of feedback, we can help ourselves by encouraging the giver to use some of the above skills. We can also help ourselves by following the guidelines below.

Guidelines for Receiving Feedback

1. **Listen to the feedback rather than immediately rejecting it or arguing with it.**

   Feedback can be uncomfortable to receive, but we may be at a disadvantage if we do not hear what people think. However, you are entitled to your opinion, and you may choose to ignore the feedback after hearing it if you believe that it is irrelevant.

2. **Be clear about what is being said.**

   Make sure that you understand the feedback or you may not be able to use it fully. Avoid jumping to conclusions or becoming defensive.

3. **Check it out with others; don't rely on one source.**

   If we rely on only one source of feedback, we may imagine that the individual's opinion is shared by everybody. We may find that other people view us differently, and this can keep the feedback in perspective.

4. **Ask for feedback that you want but don't receive.**

   We may have to ask for feedback if it is not volunteered. Sometimes the feedback we get may be restricted to one aspect of our behavior and we have to request additional feedback that we would find useful.

5. **Decide what you will do as a result of the feedback.**

   We can use feedback to help our own development. When we receive it, we can assess its value and the consequences of ignoring it or using it. Finally, we can decide what we will do as a result of it.

   Always thank the person who provided the feedback. We could benefit from it, and remember that it may not have been easy for the person to give.

Now consider the above suggestions for receiving feedback; could you work on one or two of them to improve the feedback you get? Are any of them particularly relevant to your situation or to your behavior when receiving feedback? Use the space below to write down what actions you intend to take.

The areas I need to work on when receiving feedback are

_____

_____

Summary

Giving and receiving feedback is not easy, and, more often than not, nobody enjoys either situation. Following these guidelines will make both easier and can help to prevent either from developing into a conflict situation.

The next chapter deals with the subject of conflict and how to manage it.

7

Discussions and Arguments: Managing Conflict

The objective of this chapter is to understand the causes of conflicts and to find constructive methods for resolving them.

It often is difficult to tell the difference between a discussion and an argument. Sometimes it has to do with perception; the person who is presenting his or her point of view may see it as a discussion while the other person sees it as an argument. All too often, a conversation will turn into a conflict as one person loses control of the situation, followed by the other.

This chapter introduces five negotiating skills for managing conflict in our daily lives. These are basic skills of communication and assertiveness, which need to be developed and practiced. The exercising of any kind of skill is a deliberate process. Clear thinking plays a vital part; emotional involvement is less important as one cannot think clearly in a rush of self-pity or anger.

This does not necessarily mean that, having completed this chapter of the book, you will be able to manage any conflict situation or that you will suddenly be capable of keeping calm in any circumstance! Rather, it will give you the skills necessary to handle the matter when the need arises.

It is important to be aware that, even if we are adept at using them, these skills may not work because

- It takes two to resolve a conflict.

- People may not respond to what is basically assertive behavior with assertive behavior themselves. Someone who responds passively or aggressively opts out of the problem-solving process, and you are on your own.

Having a basic knowledge of conflict-management skills will give you more of a chance more of the time and leave you feeling that you did your best.

How Do You Feel About Conflict?

In the box below write all of the words that describe how you feel about conflict. Do it quickly, without thinking too much.

The way you feel about conflict impacts the way you handle it. Do you keep your head when you are under pressure or under attack? Are you a sulker, an exploder, or a negotiator? Do you simmer, blow, or run away? It helps to know our own behavioral patterns so that we can modify our reactions in order to handle ourselves better.

Write in the box that follows any words that come to mind as you think of yourself in a conflict situation.

Now ask someone who knows you well to verify the accuracy of these statements. This person may be able to add a few more words to the list!

What Are the Causes of Conflict?

Conflict can be classified by looking at its causes.

Conflict Is a Difference of...

Interests

A disagreement between a customer and a shop owner about how much a particular item should cost may be a conflict of interests: a difference between what each one wants out of the transaction.

Understanding

I believe that you are quiet because you are sulking, but actually you are being quiet because you feel ill. This is a conflict of understanding because there is a difference between what I believe and what you know is true.

Values

An argument between two people about whether to give money to a street person is a conflict of values. It is important to one person to give money to someone who is less fortunate, and it is important to the other person that money is not given to someone without any provision for how it will be spent.

Style

A conflict caused by one person who wants to shop slowly and methodically (with a list and plenty of time to spare) and the other person who wants to do it quickly and at the last minute (in order to waste as little time as possible on it) is a conflict of style.

Opinion

I think game shows on television are good entertainment, and you think that they are boring and a terrible waste of time. This is a conflict of opinion.

Conflict Log

Try to think of three conflict situations where you have either been directly involved or where you have been an observer. Write down the situations and what the conflicts were about. Then try to classify the causes of conflicts in the terms outlined above (interests, understanding, values, style, and opinion). It is a good idea to choose simple conflict situations that contain one issue per situation.

Situation 1

The issue

The cause of conflict

Situation 2

The issue

The cause of conflict

Situation 3

The issue

The cause of conflict

Conflict Resolution

There are three basic ways of dealing with conflict:

- Aggressively—fight it
- Passively—duck it
- Assertively—negotiate

Look at the words you used at the beginning of this chapter about conflict and about your behavior in a conflict situation. Which of the ways listed above do you think is generally your style?

If yours is instinctively the "negotiate it" style of behavior, you will find developing negotiating skills relatively easy. However, most of us tend to behave either passively or aggressively, which means that we have to work a little harder to achieve a win-win resolution!

The Five Skills of Negotiation

1. Spot It

If you don't spot a conflict situation early enough, it becomes more difficult to manage. Spotting conflict is not as easy as it sounds, partly because it is sometimes the result of poor communication and misunderstanding, which is not obvious at first. Secondly, a situation can escalate very quickly once we are caught up in it. Perhaps we have been too involved to notice when it started or, for those of us who tend to be aggressive, perhaps we simply didn't want to stop!

Write down under the headings that follow some of the verbal and nonverbal behaviors that might provoke conflict.

Verbal Behavior	**Nonverbal Behavior**
(The way *words* are used.)	(The way *actions* are used.)
_____	_____
_____	_____
_____	_____
_____	_____

We thought of

- Verbal behavior: insults, sarcasm, slow emphasis, complaint, challenge, refusal, denial, shouting.

- Nonverbal behavior: door slamming, pouting, laughing inappropriately, becoming violent, becoming very quiet, growing restless and agitated, leaving the room.

You may have thought of many more; there are many ways in which people will provoke others.

Once you have spotted conflict approaching, proceed to Step 2.

2. Understand It

Look back at the situations you listed earlier in the chapter and use one of them to identify what the problem was. You have already identified the underlying cause, so pinpointing the elements will not be too difficult. There is usually more than one point of conflict in any situation. To be able to resolve it, we need to develop the skill of understanding the other person's point of view.

What are the different points of view in the situation you have chosen?

First person's points of view

1 _____
2 _____
3 _____

Other person's points of view

1 _____
2 _____
3 _____

3. Look for a Win/Win Solution

Being sensitive to conflict clues and understanding the other person's point of view is important, but choosing the appropriate way to manage it is crucial. You can decide on one of three strategies. You can decide to:

- Do something and look for the win-win (there is a win-win solution to most conflicts);
- Do something and end up with a win-lose solution, in which someone ends up having "lost"; or you can
- Do nothing. Sometimes this is appropriate and the situation resolves itself; however, it is well to double-check that you haven't just ducked the issue.

The ultimate goal of negotiation is to settle an argument leaving both people feeling that he or she has won—or, less idealistically, leaving neither feeling that he or she has lost.

Using one of the situations you chose earlier, can you think of three different outcomes, based on the three ways of dealing with it?

Win-win _____

_____

Win-lose _____

_____

Do nothing _____

_____

Once you have decided on the way that you will deal with it, you will need to:

4. Act at the Right Time

The key to this skill is to stand back long enough to answer three important questions. You need to ask yourself:

- Does this matter enough to me?
- Do I have time to act on it?
- Is this the right time to act?

Finding a win-win solution requires cool thinking, collaboration, and calmness.

The best time to act, of course, is before the conflict begins, which is why you need to develop the first skill of spotting it. However, once you are in the situation, you will need to keep control of your emotions in order to be able to think clearly. Trying to see the other person's point of view sometimes can help you keep your mind off your own emotions, and it gives you time to ask the appropriate questions.

5. Check It Out

When you have used the last four skills and have managed to reach a win-win resolution, it is important to check it out, either by going over the ground again yourself or by asking the other person involved whether he or she felt comfortable with the solution.

Personal Project

Use the following questionnaire to evaluate and analyze your skills in the next conflict situation in which you find yourself. By doing this, you will be able to pinpoint the areas that you need to work on.

The Check-It-Out Questionnaire

1. When was your conflict?
2. Who was it with?
3. What was it about? (Briefly describe the argument.)
4. What were the causes? Was the conflict because of a difference of: a. **Interests** (the difference between what you wanted and what the other person wanted)
b. **Understanding** (the difference between what you understood and what the other person understood)
c. **Values** (the difference between what is important to you and what is important to the other person)
d. **Style** (the difference between the way that you do things and the way that the other person does things)
e. **Opinion** (the difference between what you think and what the other person thinks)
Place a check mark in the appropriate box and write the actual cause (e.g., "Sue likes to dress in brilliant colors and with lots of makeup, and I hate the way that this draws attention to us").
5. Style of response. How did you react? Did you: a. Feel angry and show it?
b. Feel angry but be afraid to show it?
c. Feel angry by realizing that you would have to talk calmly about it?
6. Is this your usual reaction to conflict?
7. Did this style of response leave you feeling good: a. About yourself?
b. About the other person?

8. Negotiating the conflict.
When you spotted the conflict, what did you actually say to the other person?

9. a. Did you understand clearly what the other person's point of view was?

b. If not, what did you do to find out?

c. If you did nothing, why?

10. Did you:
a. Want to win the argument and beat the other person?

b. Know that you would lose, so there was no point trying?

c. Look for a way to have no losers?

11. Did you:
a. Jump right in with your argument or response?

b. Pause to think before speaking?

c. Let too much time go by before replying?

12. a. At the end of the conflict did you feel good or bad ? Describe your mood.

b. Did the other person feel good or bad at the end? Describe what you think was his or her mood.

13. Who won?
a. You?

b. Him/her?

c. Both of you?

Summary

In this chapter you have been introduced to the following skills of negotiation:

- Spot it
- Understand it
- Look for a win-win solution
- Act at the right time
- Check it out

When you have checked out your next conflict situation using the questionnaire, you will know where your weak points are and you will be able to work on improving them.

I still need to work on _____

_____

_____

8

Making Contact

The objective of this chapter is to practice face-to-face communication skills.

Communication involves contact with other people. Becoming skillful at communicating requires opportunities to practice the skills with other people. This chapter suggests activities that will help you to do this. Some of them you will need to do with another person; others are best done in a small group of four to six people.

If you are studying at home, think about opportunities you might have so that you can work on these activities with other people. If you are using this book at work, ask a member of the training staff or human resources department to arrange opportunities for group work.

Option 1

Watching how other people communicate can help us to improve our own skills. Use the checklist on the next page to observe other people's communication skills and to practice the ones listed.

Personal Project

You can use the checklist in various ways. For example:

1. Watch a television program that has two people involved in a conversation or discussion. A talk show or question-and-answer format is good. Observe the

Observer's Communication Checklist

Sender

- ☐ Seemed to have decided what to say
- ☐ Spoke clearly
- ☐ Varied his/her voice
- ☐ Presented one idea at a time
- ☐ Looked at the other person from time to time
- ☐ Gave examples
- ☐ Paused to allow time for questions
- ☐ Summarized to help the other person to understand
- ☐ Treated the other person with respect
- ☐ Provided verbal as well as nonverbal messages

Receiver

- ☐ Kept eye contact with the speaker
- ☐ Faced the other person, seemed relaxed and open
- ☐ Did not interrupt
- ☐ Asked relevant questions
- ☐ Seemed interested
- ☐ Seemed to recognize the other person's feelings
- ☐ Was not critical, impatient, or bored
- ☐ Sat or stood still
- ☐ Spoke clearly
- ☐ Did not "take over" the exchange
- ☐ Summarized at the end

sender and receiver and check the items on the questionnaire as you note them.
2. Arrange with your manager or training specialist to sit in on an interview or meeting between two people at work. Use the checklist to observe the participants.
3. Work with two other people. Each one of you will choose a topic to talk on for five minutes. Each one will take a turn in the following roles:

- Sender: talking about the topic;
- Receiver: listening carefully to what the other person has to say; and
- Observer: using the checklist to watch and listen to the skills of the sender and receiver.

Topics to talk about could be

- The job of my dreams;
- If I won a million dollars in the lottery;
- The best/worst things about where I live; or
- Violence and vandalism and what should be done about them.

This version may be useful if you spend a lot of your time giving instructions or directing other people. Each person should take a turn as sender, receiver, and observer, but instead of choosing a topic, each sender has to give very careful instructions about how to carry out a particular task, such as how to

- Wire a plug
- Make a skirt
- Prepare a curry dish
- Find a computer file
- Change a tire

If you prefer, choose a task at work or at home about which you often need to give instructions.

Take about ten minutes at the end of the exercise to exchange constructive feedback.

Option 2

This is an activity for three or four people.

Personal Project

Each person should spend three or four minutes preparing to give his or her views on a controversial topic, e.g., capital punishment should be brought back; women's liberation is a good idea; religion is out of date; abortion should be available on demand.

Begin with the first person, who should speak to the rest of the group for about three minutes. The second person should then summarize the first person's views and briefly reply, giving his or her own views on the subject. The second person then speaks for three minutes, giving his or her point of view on a different topic. The third person then summarizes, replies, and so on. When the last person has spoken, the first person should summarize what the last person said and reply, giving his or her views.

After doing this, discuss the following questions as a group and make notes in the space provided.

How easy is it to listen accurately to what another person is saying?

_____
_____
_____

How easy is it to listen when you have things you want to say? What might be the consequences of *not* listening?

Is it helpful to hear a summary of points you have made? If so, how?

How is communication in a group more difficult than communication between two people?

In your discussion, you may have been reminded of some of the points we made previously about distortion. It is easy to be distracted from listening accurately if you have other things on your mind or are eager to say something yourself. Summarizing is a helpful way of focusing accurately on what the sender is communicating. It gives the sender feedback about whether the message has been understood, and it helps the receiver to listen for what is important in the message.

Communication in a group is often more difficult because the sender is communicating with several receivers. Groups are made up of individuals, and each individual has a different background, experiences, and thoughts. Each person may find different meanings in the messages they receive from the sender.

Option 3

This option offers an opportunity to think about an area that you find difficult to discuss with a particular person. It is an activity for four to six people.

Personal Project

Working as a group, each member needs to think of at least one example of something that is difficult to talk about to someone. Here are some examples to prompt you. Add examples from your group in the space provided.

It Is Difficult to Talk About...	To...
Being out of work	People who think that unemployed people don't want to work
Sex	Your sexual partner
Wanting a job	An employer
Things that you are worried about or afraid of	Someone who expects you to be strong
Wanting to break off a relationship	The person with whom you have a relationship
Frustrations or difficulties in your job	Your boss or colleagues
Your Own Examples	

Now as a group spend about twenty minutes discussing the examples you have chosen, using the following questions to help you:

- Why is this topic difficult?
- Is it difficult for everybody?

- In what ways could good communication help in this situation?
- What would be the anxieties of the sender and receiver in this situation?

Summary

Now that you have worked through this program about interpersonal communication, the simplest way to summarize what you have discovered is the following diagram, which illustrates the model of face-to-face communication that we have been exploring.

A Model of Communication

Sender— the person who wants to communicate something

Relationship

Receiver— the person who becomes open to receiving the sender's message

has

has

Objectives or Purposes
- to inform
- to find out
- to persuade
- to share
- to organize
- to supervise
- to negotiate
- to protest
- to achieve
- to change, etc.

Common Interests

Individuals' Own Interests

Individuals' Own Interests

Objectives or Purposes
- to learn
- to assess
- to share
- to cooperate
- to comply
- to negotiate
- to understand, etc.

uses

uses

Sending Skills
- verbal
- nonverbal

Context— time, place, sex, age and relationship of speakers, etc.

Receiving Skills
- verbal
- nonverbal

Outcomes or Results— common or individual objectives achieved or compromise reached

Action Plan

Now that you have completed this self-study program on face-to-face communication, look back over the original objectives, including those that you may have set yourself. Have you achieved them? Now that you have worked through a number of tasks to help you increase your skills in communicating, how will you apply them? Use the space that follows to draw up an action plan for yourself.

Two things I already do well when I communicate with other people are

1 _____
2 _____

Two things I do that may hinder communication and that I will try to avoid are

1 _____
2 _____

Three things I can do to improve my effectiveness as a sender

1 _____
2 _____
3 _____

Three things I can do to improve my effectiveness as a receiver

1 _____
2 _____
3 _____

We hope that you have enjoyed working through this book. From time to time, you may want to look back through the exercises, perhaps to refresh your memory and brush up on your communication skills. You won't need to do all the exercises again as you will have learned a great deal already. We hope you enjoy putting your new skills into action!

About the Authors

Dr. Barrie Hopson

Barrie is joint chairman of Lifeskills Learning Ltd. Previously he founded the Counseling and Career Development Unit at Leeds University and was the first director until 1984. He has worked widely as a consultant to industrial and educational organizations in the United Kingdom, the United States of America, and Europe. He was responsible for setting up the first career counseling service in British industry in 1970 (at Imperial Chemical Industry) and has since helped a number of organizations in different countries to set up career counseling and career management systems. He is a professional associate of the National Training Laboratories for Applied Behavioral Science in Washington, D.C., a fellow of the British Psychological Society, and a fellow of the British Institute of Management.

He has written twenty-two books and numerous articles on personal and career development, marriage, lifeskills teaching, quality service, transition, and change management and generic training skills.

Mike Scally

Mike is joint chairman of Lifeskills Learning Ltd. He combines management training with writing and lecturing. He was Deputy Director of the Counseling and Career Development Unit at Leeds University in 1976 and was involved with its training programs and national projects until 1984.

He has extensive training experience with many of the United Kingdom's major companies and an international reputation in the field of education. He serves on the management committees of and is consultant to many national groups—promoting development education and training at home and abroad.

Mike Scally has written twelve books and many articles on career management, customer service, and lifeskills teaching.